Rough Cut

Rough Cut

. . . .

Poems by

Thomas Swiss

University of Illinois Press   *Urbana and Chicago*

This book is printed on acid-free paper.

Library of Congress Cataloging-in-Publication Data

Swiss, Thomas, 1952–
    Rough cut : poems / by Thomas Swiss.
        p.   cm.
    I. Title.
    PS3569.W575R68   1997
    811'.54—dc20   96-35656
                                            CIP

Acknowledgments

Grateful acknowledgment to the editors of the publications in which these poems first appeared:

Agni: "Hey Now"
Boston Review: "River"
Greensboro Review: "Here from There"
Cimmaron Review: "Lucky One"
Blue Mesa Review: "Mental Chess," "Walkie-Talkie"
Outerbridge: "Flood," "Sun Going Down," "Shy Boy"
The Iowa Review: "On a Stanza by Rilke"
The Nebraska Review: "In the Woods"
Third Coast: "The Problem"
The Rhetoric Review: "Rock Shop," "Boy in the Basket"
Tar River Poetry: "The Dream Life"

"On a Stanza by Rilke" also appeared in *Twice Told: Poets on Poetry* (Middlebury, Vt.: New England University Press, 1997).

Thanks to the University of Iowa Center for Advanced Studies and the Humanities Center at Drake University for their support. Special thanks to Cynthia Lewis, Steven Cramer, and Laurence Lieberman.

For Alley and Jacob

Contents

3

• • •

1

. . .

Rock Shop

She no longer loved him is what she told him.
    He should try to understand that—
        but he couldn't because she wasn't making sense.

It was as if she were talking under water. Or from a place
    so far away it hardly mattered what she said.
        Weren't they happy? Couldn't she see how happy

they were? Not like those first years, of course,
    the relationship newly minted. But nobody's rich
        like that for long—good riddance to those years!

So now what? Is he required to revisit, thanks to her,
    every stupid fight, every *I want* and *You don't get it?*
        The ground shifting, looking for clues: it makes him

want to tear his face off. And today? Today he drives
    his son to the rock shop to give himself time
        to think, to sort things out while his son browses

and chats with the owner who's all hair—full beard,
    ponytail—and who's saying in a super-loud voice:
        Check it out! And suddenly he wants to, too.

With his son, he's drawn to the rock the guy places
    in the boy's hand, as the sales pitch—half science,
        half New Age nonsense—begins. But he already knows

he's got to have it, he's going to buy it, and bring it home
    to her wrapped in tissue, and with a card that says
        just the right thing. If she doesn't understand?

. . .

3

He'll explain it to her. And if she still doesn't get it?
No problem. This is how the rock was cut, he'll say;
this explains its colors; and that, its textures; its age,

more or less, its place of origin—careful to get his facts
correct, careful not to give her anything she might
change or challenge when it's her turn to speak.

. . .

Hey Now

One day, then, soon after she'd left him, he knew it was time
to examine his feelings, time to look hard
at what he felt,

and what he could do about it. Do? Truth is he didn't feel like
doing anything. But the trees that had been dying
all fall without him—

suddenly they seemed to have something to say,
and suddenly it was his job
to listen. Fine,

he didn't mind listening. It's just that it wasn't his strength.
So when he stood at the window,
it was a gesture

of faith, though he believed, of course, he'd be disappointed,
that nothing would come of it, not one
thing. Like his friend's visit:

what did it prove? Last night the two of them talking and drinking,
then shouting as if they weren't scared,
but brave: Down

the hatch! Down the fucking hatch! All right, so this wouldn't be
easy. He'd have to give up feeling stupid
or numb, he'd have

to wait here for instructions. And the trees said: *Hey now.*
Hey now? Was that it? And the trees said:
How about learning

. . .

a little patience? Because nobody believes you the first time
you say that you'll
change.

. . .

The Problem

I stay busy. That's not the problem. I work late,
I go to movies. But mostly, I guess, I rehearse.
And that's where I met her, where I first met

her friends—at the Ingersoll Dinner Theater.
Like sex when you know it's the last thing
you need, but you go on chasing it anyway—

that's how we got together. At first it wasn't much:
drinks and some awkward self-conscious talk
in a bar down the street. Then things escalated.

I remember I was walking her back to her car—
it must have been two or three nights later—
when she started telling me she'd had

her breasts done, and whipped up her shirt
to show me. Man! I suppose, when I think about it,
I should have seen that as some kind of clue.

But I didn't: I was too vain and needy. And her?
Worse. Calling on the phone or coming over—
I mean pretty soon my whole life was her,

and I couldn't do anything else. It was always
Listen, I have to talk, and I heard the urgency,
I heard a desperation in her voice that hooked me.

But at the theater, she was having problems, and it
wasn't only me who noticed. We were getting
toward the end of rehearsals—everybody gets kind

. . .

of loony then, anyway—and she'd be screw-
ing up her lines. Lines she'd said fine for weeks.
Like *Oh, God! That's what I love about Iowa.*

They roll up the sidewalks after dinner. That's not
a tough one, but when she got hold of it, there was
no way it was coming out right. *Lord God!*

she'd say, *what I like about Iowa,* and then,
catching herself, she'd start over: *Oh, God!
That's what Iowa.* . . . and it wasn't funny

like you might think, it wasn't like those
bloopers on TV. The cast, including me,
was getting pissed. I'd met her friends by then:

Michael, Lorna, some guy she called Tiger.
They had a special language, like friends
sometimes do. If you were being goofy,

you were "on a drive." If you were stressed
or couldn't cope, you weren't able to "fold
your napkin." And if you said or did something

that went too far, one of them would
say—usually in wide-eyed mock disbelief—
"honey, the rant runneth over." Finally,

we opened at the Ingersoll, and luck
was with us all. No flubbed lines, nobody sick,
no malfunctioning props or surprises. Even

the newspaper ran a flattering piece about us.
The last time the two of us went out, we saw
a movie the community college was showing:

The Blue Angel with Marlene Dietrich.
Remember how it starts out funny? Then
the next thing you know it's vicious,

•   •   •

it's sparing you nothing. And the scene
at the end—when the magician breaks an egg
over the guy's bald head so the yolk runs down

his face, and he starts crying like a rooster, *cock-*
a-doodle-do! and the camera won't turn away.
Next to me in that big lecture hall they use

as a theater on weekends, I could feel her
shrinking, and then whispering from her seat:
Please, please, end this scene. But the camera

refused to blink: the rant runneth over. And
we both knew—even before the lights came
back on—that whatever we'd done to or kept

from each other didn't matter now. It was
done. We were free, and it was OK
to say so, if only we could find the words.

. . .

Stupid Moon

Dropping her cigarette and a full cup of beer,
she tripped over the chair

someone had wedged between tables.
She was tired, unmistakably,

but edgy, too. Scrambled. Ready for something.
Sure, I should have stopped her—

not that I cared. But suddenly she was up there
shouting at the singer . . .

Poor guy,
putting his hands on the mike—the way friends

have put theirs over her mouth to keep her from getting punched.
You're dirt, she's screaming.

Isn't that how it is? The style of the drinker's concentration—
a voice inside her voice,

a light drilling through her, a fire
fanning her brain . . .

Only then the bouncer ran over. Come on,
sit down, I should have said,

it's almost closing time.
But somebody yelled: *Get her out of here, man.*

So I did. And we walked home,
ducking the headlights, cursing the stupid moon.

• • •

10

To Explain

To explain the argument that leaves them shaken—
in the bedroom, crying
and late for work,

exhausted, half-dressed, red-faced—I'd have to but really can't bear to
say more. Who wants
to hear it?

Do you?
More about her problem and how it drove her,
and then the requisite lying

and sadness.
Then this.
It started with a piece of paper, I know, something she'd written on,

meant to toss,
forgot, and then he found it. Now neither of them wants to touch
this thing

that closes with a dash and three big Xs, kisses canceled with a slash.
But, no,
she's not looking

to call it off, to retreat, to apologize, she's not looking
to save face. Are you
listening? You

there—
if she asks,
should he offer his pity? Forgiveness? Is it too late for these now?

. . .

Now the clock on the desk says Continue. The bed sheets, books
on the floor. The ocean
of clouds

receding
from the window: Go On, they say,
Continue. How

can I, knowing—don't you, don't *you?*—how this argument ends.

. . .

At the Center for Chemical Dependency

It's catching. I go there, and I walk the grounds
with her, and we talk politely, until, slowly
and very quietly, we tell each other the truth, completely.

Do I hear violins? She's discovered a courtyard,
five crosshatched sidewalks filled with a confusion
of phrases, doodles, names. Done in swirling neon chalk strokes,

this must be somebody's project, somebody's self-
saving in-process art composed under Therapy's sign.
But what sponsors Patience, authorizes Luck?

From the fourth floor window, from her room, these markings
remind her of the story a clever man told the tabloids:
his aerial photos, some doctored shots of scrapings

in the desert, were evidence of runways, proof the Ancients
had been visited by spacecraft. Every age
has its ideas, its rigorous and farfetched interpretations . . .

Here the aliens have all crash-landed, drifted back in
from their distant orbits, dysfunctional families,
asked to confess, reminisce, repent. One day it's out

with the old ways of thinking: blot, blot, blot. Another day
it's retouch with a decorator's brush. Her blonde
session-mate calls it Healing the Soul,

though to her it's both more and less abstract—
like tuning a piano under water.
Better not to worry it now, or let the future hurry

. . .

our stroll as the sun warms these sidewalks we're careful
to walk around, not wanting to walk over the orange
half-sentence that says clearly, curiously: Big Secrets from Sally.

A message recovered from the unrecovered, it means nothing
to the rain which will wash it away. Then the visit was over
once more, and because I knew she wanted me to, I told her I loved her.

.   .   .

Faith

Glasses surrendered with her car keys and clothes—
still the trick's to focus,

to call to mind a scene that's ripe for dreaming.
Not the abstract splash of sky, glimpsed from a faraway window,

but the near-at-hand, the extreme close-
up. The doctor gave her a spinal. He asked her to lean,

to raise her hands up over the pillow,
over the cool white pillow. Like a lake, only shallow.

Only then she's over her head in it: faith
in the dubbed voice of the nurse, rising through her forgetting.

. . .

In the Vending Room

Allied, Hawkeye, Co-Op,
Wayne's Feeds—

she's trying to remember
if the optical shop was on 13th Street or not.

Her friend thinks he knows, but he wants confirmation.
Hawkeye, Co-Op,

Wayne's—she's trying. Trying, but something's not right.
There's a buzzing in her head she can't override,

a space she keeps drifting into . . .
Thus she draws on her cigarette: Give me a minute,

will you? To which her friend replies:
Take the whole day

if you want to. Sure.
Like he means it! Yeah. Ha-ha. As if

he didn't care or weren't already angry,
and this break went forever,

and work meant nothing. As if she were
herself again: ha-ha.

. . .

16

Ampersand

Everybody had to run around like crazy to get what it was
she wanted. About four
in the morning, she decided she wanted a chocolate milkshake—

In literature, in life, in the reading of corresponding texts,
to connect, what else is there?,
to make sense of, to get something from or out of,

—with two scoops of ice cream and a blob of something else.
She was frantic to get out. She responded
to that place like a frenzied animal. At all cost, at any cost,—

to stipulate as authority stipulates, not the surface
structures of change taking place,
not only what's manifested in, but what manifests, not the reception,

—she was going to call the cops. She was going to call
the board of directors, whoever she knew,
she was going to get out of that place that day.—

not only the reception, but the practice and production
of art, philosophy, propaganda.
The dominating symbol: an immense ampersand

in neon pink, superimposed onto a kind of montage
in which various images and forms
are overlaid in the style of the day. It belongs to the lingua franca—

. . .

—After she left the hospital, she said: I have an accident
every two years, — of cultural symbols
in the bedroom or boardroom, in the salon, and it proclaims—

and one day, I can tell you right now, it won't be an accident.

. . .

18

Mr. Romance

Flush with cash from six months working—
but I don't want to talk about that awful job.
In this life begun after getting over you,

I'd rather remember what the money bought us.
That flat with a rented view of *our* England:
17 Wakeman Road. Gone there to make something

for ourselves, an itch that lifted us over the ocean
with two backpacks, books, and a carton of Kools.
Gone there, hoping to sidestep Nixon.

Sweethearts, artists: how could we lose?
What we needed was time, and there was plenty.
Afternoons, painting while our neighbors

hung their washing on the grid of ropes
outside our window. Remember those voices?
They echoed in the courtyard, their brightness

far-reaching, while upstairs we eavesdropped,
and worked in corners of the same room.
It seemed so easy, of course I wanted it to go on forever,

but soon a whole year passed. It was time
to go home. In those last days, we talked about
what we'd missed: Oxford and Liverpool had been

on our list before the strikes shut the railways.
And Ireland—well, after the bombings . . .
On the down escalator, in the Nottingham mall,

. . .

we talked about what we'd do when we returned.
But you were lying. You were wearing your new
platform shoes, Mr. Vain. Mr. Romance, towering

over me, already out of reach. Don't think I forgive you.

. . .

2

. . .

In the Woods

Come in, say the trees, *deeper* in,
but my father doesn't want to.

He's tired, he says, he's not feeling
up to it. And, really,

that's OK. The trees are just asking:
they have what they need.

They have all the time in the world.
And this girl resting on the grass

by the river—
what about her? As if life were based on

or copied from art, she reads a book,
listens to her portable stereo . . .

My father's been ill for six months now.
He's tired all the time.

The tug of his inwardness—
I know it's bitter. He doesn't want to go

deeper. And this girl
who travels

by plugging herself in:
what does she know? Rubbing

a shoulder, brushing her hair,
turning another page . . .

.   .   .

Will you do me a favor, My Fiction,
My Lie? Teach my father

to argue with the trees. And with the river
that says there is no elsewhere—

only revision and then the ellipsis.

. . .

For Sale by Owner

When I think of my father as a young man, I imagine him
at his job stocking groceries at Carl's on Cicero Street.
He must be about eighteen. And he must be thinking about the war,

like everyone else alive then. It rained in Chicago
most of that summer, rained on the sidewalks and storefront
awnings, on the tanklike cars cruising the corner,

and the grown-ups come to shop with their coupons, the kids
buying baseball cards. People still dreamed, of course,
but everything was dyed the same sepia: like those newspapers

he lugged in a bundle from the curb with their heart-stopping,
24-point headlines. When I think of him now,
I see him sweeping up a jar of yellow mustard some kid in a cart

knocked over. In an apron his mother had pressed that morning,
down on his knees, mopping the mess into a heavy dustpan . . .
Then it's eight months later: he's in his army uniform,

eating lunch with some buddies in a hangar in Europe. Click.
Of all the images my mother's saved of my father, only this one
hangs on a wall. My mother didn't know him when this photo

was taken—maybe that explains why she values it,
this life she can only imagine, with its promises intact.
At seventy, their lives are not so bad, but not great either:

their health declining, their house up for sale, the house
I lived in for twenty years, and have come back to help pack.
All these things they've kept for reasons no one remembers!

.   .   .

25

These leftovers from the new Machine Age, its different aesthetic—
a Nouveau-style tin of Hi-Hat face cream; a jar of Jerry's
tooth powder; a beat-up board game, Tek-No-Crazy,

with robots on the box. What to do with them? My parents
are moving to a condo soon. It's the kind of place
with a kitchenette and only a locker in the basement for storage.

It's near a small downtown in the suburbs; happily, it's close
to my sister's. When I think of my father in his apron
or uniform, when I think of my young mother, but there's work

to do, and I'm only in for the weekend. And these leftovers—
is that too harsh of a word?—these mementos, antiques,
artifacts—some in beautiful colors, period greens and cobalt

blues. I want to be finished with them. Like the flywheels
and fan belts from a time both glamorous
and Xed out now, they have almost no place left in the world.

. . .

Go

By then he had gone
so far into himself,
he could no longer hear the crying.

Nor the voices,
hushed,
those calling him back: Sharon's
and Michael's. Suzanne's.

The medicines?
He was done with them.
He was done with the injections.

It was like stabbing somebody, Suzanne says.
Then she says:
but this waiting is worse.

In the mornings,
lying on her mother's bed now,
reading
while the phone goes unanswered—

beyond the fog of disbelief,
beyond the next stage and the next, to this:
she's given him
her permission.

That's what
the night nurse told her:
they each had to say it to make him go.

.   .   .

They had to bend down right next to his bed
and say it.

So that the flowers on the nightstand
could simply be flowers—
emptied of meaning, like the water glass.

. . .

Spilled It

You want to know
    how I feel
        about my father?
When I was a kid,
    he called me
        French Fry.
Later, it was Steamboat
    or Lulu. Lu-
        lu! Just
say he was like that.
    He liked funny
        names. Stagy names.

That night in Chicago,
    I think I spilled it
        all out:
didn't you feel it?
    The whole story.
        That's why
I can't come back
    to it now.
        I said it:
it's gone. I don't have
    the energy
        to be with him

like that, not even
    at mother's house
        anymore. But
that night in the hotel bar
    in Chicago,
        I told you

. . .

all about him, and the drink
    sat there, and
        the cigarette
sat there. It was scary,
    he came back
        so hard. After

I went to the bathroom,
    I didn't feel
        well—could you
tell?—but I looked
    across the table,
        and the drink
was half gone,
    and the cigarette
        was still lit
and smoking. And
    I swear it, my father
        was there.

. . .

Night Ride Home

After the argument,
my sister cried.
In the back
seat in winter, in a car
headed home,
because
she could not let it go.
Because the hours
refused
to be hurried: my father
driving,
my mother
driving, gas, no gas, ice.
She did not
know
not to carry her anger —
like our Buick
dragging
its flattened shadow,
tugging it
into the night.
And the back shelf
crowded
with souvenirs,
and the map my mother
scanned
with a penlight,
fished from the bottom
of her purse . . .
Nobody
spoke then, nobody
spoke. But
the snow

.   .   .

began falling, and changed
   the subject
      because the moon
withdrew. Like you,
   Suzanne, gone
      back into the book
  you were reading . . .

. . .

Mental Chess

Wanna try it? That's my brother, calling from the other bed,
asking me to play the game he's invented. He's king of the house,
my brother: older, quieter, doer of crosswords, reader of serious books . . .

Not that I cared or really thought much about him. Like my desk
piled high with baseball cards, the lump in my mattress,
the light that burned all night in the hall—he was just there,

a condition of childhood. Now, above the whir of the machine
that filtered pollen as it hummed all summer on our floor,
my brother was explaining the rules. It's like regular chess, he says,

except we do it in our heads. You know: no board.
No board? What was he saying? I could hardly play the real thing
during the day. But he had already begun, announcing his first move

in a voice so solemn I thought he was joking. And whatever
I'd managed to bring to mind vanished then, so that
when it was my turn, I was silent a long time until finally

my brother asked if I was sleeping. Not exactly, I thought,
lying in the dark, embarrassed and angry at myself. And at him
who nobody could touch. Like the woman I'd seen in the park that day,

bending to drink from a fountain while her boyfriend held the handle . . .
But which figure was me? Which did I want to be? Even
with my eyes closed, I could tell what my brother was doing then—

turning off his reading light with a sock so he wouldn't get burned.

. . .

The Dream Life

Then there was the time
I saw the flying saucer:
blinking, blurred,
sunlit above a ditch.

When our car came closer,
I saw it was
a rusting bumper
or something thrown

from the back of a truck
as it bumped up over the hill.
The dream life?
It comes to nothing—

an angel, a childhood tree.
And looking back now,
there is always that evening
when Father stood next to me

at the window,
toasting the Fourth of July.
That was a waterfall, he said,
as the fireworks exploded.

He spoke to my reflection
swimming in the glass:
Did you see the waterfall?
But it was a flower I saw,

. . .

the petals dimming into night.
In the darkened room,
he reached for the light,
erasing us both in an instant.

. . .

Walkie-Talkie

That tape-box from a talking doll, the Heath Kit stereo,
  anything with wires,
                    tubes or transistors—

we loved and broke them all. But not our walkie-talkies.
  Nights, in our rooms,
                    we played at being deejays,

singing the Monkees, Beatles, Byrds. That's what
  I remember. And talking
                    too much: our words spliced

to static, awash with others' in a stratosphere complete
  with coded beeps and buzzes. And when
                    one of us grew sleepy,

both of us signed off: that's what I remember. And once,
  when I woke,
                    I thought I heard you calling—

but was it *you* calling me across those big back yards?
  You, if I had answered then,
                    who would have spoken

back again? Or was it only a local ham, or one from among
  the order of truckers
                    whose nightly blabbing

I resented? Do you remember, neighbor? Dreamer
  or dreamed one, voice that held me
                    at the glass: *Dave to Thom,*

it whispered, then hushed. *Dave to Thom,* it repeated.

• • •

Bragging Rights

The boy begging a quarter in the parking lot
outside the St. Charles Y—

what did he know about me?
Or was his asking impersonal? An excuse to get something

going. Anyone
can tell you part of this story,

tell you he was hitched to the wrong future already—
before hitting me full in the face with his fist,

before he'd ever hit anyone. For my part, I swear:
I never saw it coming. His punches arriving in super-slow-motion,

then in sped-up cartoon fashion: Pow! Whack!
A horrible dreamlike hyper-alertness. Then it was over,

and I was still drunk. I'd gone there to hear
the local bands play covers,

to dance with my friends as I did every Friday,
all of us in stocking feet

in the gym, tipsy in the strobe that encouraged our posing.
But after the hours slipped by inconclusively?

Only the chaos of wading, past midnight,
though piles of mismatched shoes . . .

I never saw it coming. His buddies
must have—

. . .

two of them leaning on the wood-paneled car
I described to my parents later.

Later, when my father said *This is what happens,*
and I knew what he meant, for once.

I'd hung out in that lot dozens of times,
or crossed it with friends

on the way to play pool at a table where the hours were banked,
the days sunk. Sure, I wanted to get something

going. And the boy?
What might that boy have said about himself?

Or felt but refused to say. To me,
his knowledge was of another order,

so whatever
I might have learned from him

never could have mattered.
At the dance we ignored the chaperons, the rented policeman

who yawned by the door,
who dusted us out to the locked-down streets

where more than one of us walked home barefoot—
stoned or stupid or on a dare—and the next day,

embarrassed, headed back.
Regretful Cinderellas. Like mine,

the boy's fantasies demanded detail. Anyone can tell you.
But, please,

you tell me: when I remember lying there,
sprawled on the gravel,

. . .

what can I do—what am I *supposed* to do—
but let him go again?

. . .

City of Men

1.

The eight-foot blow-up Frankenstein balloon
    I'd won in a carton of cola—
every few years I unbury this picture
    with others I've saved
for—what?—looking, I guess. And
    telling, too: I was nine
when my parents moved us. *Stole* us
    from the frontiers of post-
war suburbia to an old river town
    whose name meant City
of Lights.

       At first, not much seemed
to shine. Later,
    a few things: like trips
to my father's office on Saturdays.
    Nine until noon,
washing his windows: bucket after
    bucket of cold soapy
water, and then—with a final scrape
    of the squeegee—

        done. So why

not head to the Paramount Theater?
    —Golden dome above a pink
marquee above a kindly man
    who slipped you
your ticket and smiled. Or maybe
    walk down

. . .

to the Aurora Hotel, where once, I heard,
    only the rich stayed,
but now only the transient
    and old. Like Mr. Custer,
an old Jew who knew Esperanto,
    and who sat
in my father's optometrical office,
    reading and dozing
and looking—

2.

                        Sometimes
I'd go with him back to his "home."
    What was it about
that place? The smudged glass
    doors, the low-voltage lobby
where the men smoked, playing cards,
    the bar a few yards
from the untended front desk, and—

    there it is—still shining,

the sign: the one
    hanging half out
the window. Electric, flicked on
    even during the day,
it said what it said in blue neon—

                ROOMS
        CLEAN   MEN ONLY.

3.

    What are you doing here?
someone asked—or was that only
    what I was afraid

· · ·

41

of being asked, someday and by someone
     who'd come up behind me,
catching me admiring the cigarette
     machine or racing down
the marble stairs
     to the bathroom
to stand at a urinal so tall I balanced
     on tiptoe and stared,
eye-level, at the writing on the pipe.
     It said: *Sloans.*

          New world
     of colognes and language,
new world of routines—a man, a stick-
     man, in a starched shirt
shining other men's wing tips,
     brushing
their broad or narrow
     shoulders, using a chewed-up
whisk broom. He had a strange voice:
     when he talked,
it was like a radio clicking on.
     From the men
he handed towels to, he accepted a coin,
     before they bowed
to spit or rinse their combs . . .

          And the queer graffiti
on the back of the stall door,
     the green and gray checks
on the floor I squinted at, half in a trance,
     sitting on the toilet:
the tiles cracked, speckled with red—
     was it blood?

          Everything coded, private,
male—

          who were they? These

   . . .

men in no hurry: these Fellows,
    Misters, Guys. Were some
of them gamblers? Were any fathers?

4.

Dreamy and stage-lit, distant, abstract:
    whatever I saw there
made me wish
    for safe passage.
If not into *these* lives, exactly—
    too dangerous, too sub-
terranean—then into any existence
    filled with such richly

            translatable detail.
What *was* I doing there?
    The voice was right
in asking. And its other questions:
    what did I learn? Did it help,
did it hurt whoever
    I imagined I was or could be
on these Saturdays, Saturdays,

        Saturdays—

like the one when I blew air into
    the Frankenstein
I'd won, and propped him in the window
    of my father's office. Monster-
man, Darkness Incarnate—
    I almost forgot
I was telling you about him—
    how he leaned into October's
moody sun, and amused the kids
    who came in
with their parents for glasses.
    But later, when I came back

. . .

to help my father clean, we saw
    someone had pinched
or punched him: he whispered
    an unlocatable hiss
that brought him,

        in a few hours,

              down to size—

    down to *my* size: and like me,
flabby, a threat to no one.

. . .

3

. . .

Here from There

Sheridan Harbor Island, San Diego

In each new city, a new start.
The glass door that opens
to a balcony

opens out to the harbor
and a dozen bobbing yachts,
freighters,

gunboats, and beyond them,
the city at night.
Fire on the water,

beauty has its own ways
of interrogating feeling.
In each new city,

in *this* one, two women
are walking a dog
on the beach—

their conversation
keeps loneliness at bay.
Not like the zigzag

skyline (charting the erotic
heartbeats of club-goers),
nor the rose appearing twice

a day in a bud vase
(courtesy of room service).
I pull the heavy

. . .

47

paisley curtains closed.
City of laundry, ashtrays,
gift shops,

how would you have me
collaborate?
City of after-hours TV.

Tug boats, will you meet me
part of the way,
where the seawall

divides here from there?
Seabirds. Whirring sound
I can't locate.

Cook in your tall white hat—
ducking out the back door
at midnight,

why won't you let me love you?

. . .

Poem Beginning with Lines from a Self-Help Book

It's all in the mind, that's the Age-Old secret.
Practice until you learn
to control it.
Power:

you will it, it's yours. From his bedroom,
then, from the moment his parents
go off to sleep,
the boy

controls the house. It's his: this room
with its books and animals,
its rocks and high-
tech toys,

but also the view to the street that earlier
worried him. No problem
now—it's under
his control.

And other things, too. Why not? He deserves this—
lying there, clicking a flashlight
in sync with the music
that booms

through his headphones and helps him
concentrate. His younger sister,
asleep with a tractor—
he controls

. . .

his sister's on and off snoring, he can
make her turn over by thinking
about it, and then,
for fun,

make her cough. And all the toilets flush
when he says so, the floor squeaks
when something falls
in the kitchen,

something he wished down from its shelf.
He has it all planned. The birds
that wake at 5 A.M.,
unaware

they answer to him now, unsuspecting—
those dumb birds will be his
soon. The trick is
to focus

on something—his X-men, his baseball cards—
anything to take his mind
off this feeling:
weary

one minute, unstoppable the next.
He can do it, he can will
himself to it,
he can

stay awake until the sun rises, until it orbits
under his control. Like those images
that come to him
from TV,

flickering and half-hallucinated: a girl
putting lipstick on in the mirror
or reaching for a penny
in a glass;

. . .

an old man shrugging his shoulders . . .
But all of them slip away
so quickly,
all

of them gone in a flash. Only power lasts—
the mind swallowing
its subjects
with ease

in this kingdom where no one dares to ignore him
or ask (as someone will tomorrow):
Exactly what do you think
you're doing?

  • • •

Shy Boy

It's no mystery why he presses his back to the wall
while the other children pass
from Health to Playground. He's melting,

he can't help it. And he can't help that
he's easy to read, even from this end of the hall.

You know what he wants to do? Vanish.
If he could make this difficult wish come true,
but he can't. Like the eclipse

he studies in science class, to be there and then to not be there,
like a spelling mistake the eraser undoes,

the smudge the pencil writes over.
But why not also leave some sign—
a fountain left running, the arc of water

meant for his lips suspended, untouched. Something for others
to puzzle out later, after he's stopped caring,

but he can't. I think he might as well have what he desires.
Already a ghost, see how he leans in the air
of his refusals, against the battered lockers?

. . .

River

When the river recedes, I don't ask what tamed it,
      counting from the porch

those things I thought lost: the dock in the muddy
      sunlight, bobbing;

the garden, loyal to fate. I don't ask the river why
      it changed its mind,

there—then *not* there—on the grass or on the bank
      where last year you walked

with the daughter you were leaving, and where now
      a few oxeyes

encourage her attention. Or is something else calling her?
      Body alert, mind drifting . . .

This is how she moves when she doesn't know how to,
      when she's troubled

and can't say it. With a wooden shovel, she digs
      by the birdhouse

that's home to the floating cardinal: red in this field
      of green. And there,

by the poplar branching over the river you crossed
      to the other side,

she knows what she's meant to find. You showed her.
      And you taught her

. . .

to trust in a thorny order, its tipsy give and take. Only
    now she wishes it

less abstract, wishes that the long view time provides
    might be granted her easily,

and all in one flash. Hole in her heart, where the rain
    tugs away whatever it can,

stealing it to the river—don't ask what she's doing.
    River, unhook her.

. . .

Flood

This keyboard can't take the place of his piano,
but it will do. It has to. The piano's
inaccessible, locked in a house still surrounded

by water. A summer without music: is that
how my eight-year-old son will remember it?
Will the blurry photos I saved from the city paper

bring it back? Along with certain images,
I suppose: his parents on the lawn,
consulting with neighbors; his friends

riding bicycles through the street in their swimsuits,
scaring the ducks, watching the waves
lap the curbside mailbox. What will he remember

of that first afternoon? The parked cars starting
to take on water? In one—a sturdy Volvo—
a little drama unfolded: a white purse floated

from the saturated seat, spilling its bills,
tissues, I.D.s. But I think only evening
made what was happening seem real:

the phone on the blink; the rain still falling.
Maybe that's what will stick—
his first fears surfacing, framed as questions

no one seemed able to answer. And the waiting—
with his brother, playing *Don't Break the Ice,*
tapping the little blue cubes with a hammer

. . .

55

until one of the boys misguessed, at last,
and lost, and the igloo collapsed on the table . . .
But it won't end here, whatever he recalls,

because the story doesn't end here. He sits
at the rented keyboard now: what is there
to do but practice? And between notes

the pauses suggest what he's feeling —
that whatever happens next, there will be
no forgetting. No more lapses or gaps.

. . .

Lucky One

April, in the second grade, they all brought plants
to class. Then vacation came:
waxy grass

in dime store baskets, his cousins in their bonnets.
Help him to remember,
will you?,

how that classroom changed. How after break
the sash that draped the crucifix
came down.

And wasn't he the lucky one? Asked to fold the sash
and then return it
to the shelf—

in front of all the others. But, later, when his teacher
asked how all of them
saw God,

he drew a hulking creature with two heads. Terrible
and animal, it wasn't a joke,
one head scowling

as he tried to hide it, to cover his paper
when the teacher walked the row.
But the other

had no face: it was a stone, revealing nothing.
Like the plant he'd brought
to school,

. . .

the iris that flowered no matter if he ignored it,
this creature, he knew, didn't need
him. So who did?

. . .

Recital

Bring the camera! Isn't that what she had shouted to him on her way
out the door? He'd heard her say it,

he'd even said it once or twice himself, in the shower
after she'd gone. After she'd gone, he had a minute alone—

plenty of time to forget. So when he arrived
at the mall to hear his son play piano,

he didn't have the camera. Mother and child among mothers and children—
he surveyed the scene from the escalator

on his way down—everyone hunched on folding chairs,
the kids waiting turns to ascend to the stage to play for some last-minute,

gift-bearing shoppers, who looked blankly on
while the teacher ran the show. Huge as a tree,

and in a green dress, the teacher tinkled a few duets, cued the canned music,
fiddled with a synthesizer, winked, thanked,

and applauded. Everything moving along on time; everything fine
and festive—at least in the way these things usually are,

and meaningful to those who need it. Not that he was feeling
that need. In fact, he was feeling

disconnected, having passed a small accident on his way to the mall.
Whatever had happened was almost over

by the time he crept by: an ambulance was pulling out of a ditch
where apparently someone had landed; a tow truck

. . .

was busy with a dented Camaro; a woman in a neck brace sat
in back of a cop car . . .

but he wasn't there now. He was *here*. He leaned on a pole
and tried to focus. The smell of fresh pizza,

of gourmet cookies being packed into bags behind him—
Now, he was thinking, for without his camera,

there'd be nothing to look at later. Then the tree stood
to put his son's name

in big block letters on the stand. ALLEY, it said,
and the boy came forward, clutching his notebook and music. All right,

he said to himself again,
so *this* is what life feels like. OK, he said, I can handle that.

. . .

Sun Going Down

I panicked. I admit it. I expected the worst
when the arguing couple dumped their kids
at the swings, and stormed off. Now there

was only the sun going down and bird-cries
meshed with the crunch of spun gravel:
a pale blue Nissan leaving the parking lot,

ducks hurrying out of its way . . .
They've gone off to talk it over. If only
they could get a moment out of earshot,

but somehow we all still hear them. Like a bad
headache, instantly vivid: the pain, the pauses,
the *fuck this, fuck that,* the whole predictable,

inappropriately public, passionate, lamentable,
knotty syntax lumbers back to us, while my son—
who's one and beginning to walk—tries to find

his footing. He has his own argument, bending
to gravity's bidding. In sand, through weeds,
on the lip of the empty wading pool, shifting

his weight he crab-walks, lurches, weaves
like a dog caught in traffic. See what I mean?
I needed help. I looked to the other animals:

a lion whose mouth was a crawl-through barrel,
a rusty elephant slide. Each guarding
its weedy plot, each with its appeal. Now

. . .

the woman rests on the picnic table, her right
hand protecting her head. I want to go to her,
but I can't. My son is lying in the grass,

complaining, the kids are chasing some squirrels
near the pond, and the man — her boyfriend
or husband or whatever — just stands there,

looking up at the sky. Where have our angels
all gone? And what might the sun mean to teach us,
but can't? Like me, late for my next appointment,

the sun has no time now to shelter the child
who runs toward her mother, shouting Stop! Stop!
It takes its pictures down from the walls,

the lovely and the absurd ones. Until tomorrow,
it takes even those things we claim to be ours:
not the fireflies arriving for nightfall, but the view

of this park from the hill where our home is,
where my son and I live not far from that monkey
bars' disappearing checkerboard shadow.

. . .

The Boy in the Basket

Sidelined with others his age, with the third-graders
too small or too afraid of the ball to do much good
in these early innings, the boy in a basket goes unnoticed

until it's his time to bat. Then he is there (top of
the fourth, one kid on), being wheeled out by three
of his teammates. In caps and cleats, pushing his heavy,

gleaming, metal chair, they seem in no hurry to reach
the damp field, wading through the rough grass that sets
the basket rocking. Someone who loves him must have

rigged this contraption, someone who admires this boy
for working at a game he can't altogether play.
What happens when he hits the ball? Everybody's watching,

as over our heads the sun's setting, first mosquitoes
snag the air, and the broad shadows make it hard
to see exactly how he's positioned in that thing.

I'm curious. I want to know how it works, how he's able
to stand up, what supports him in the basket
and holds the basket to the chair. Are there parents here

not drawn into pity, and then, without a gap,
into thinking about their own kids? It's creepy,
comparing problems, but right now the usual concerns—

asthma, awkwardness, the extra pounds that bring on teasing—
all seem nothing. Yet trying to picture *his* life,
I have to go back thirty years—to when the son

.   .   .

of one of my mother's friends got hit, almost killed, by a car.
Though I saw him in his chair only twice, my mother
told me stories. What was I to understand? The usual stuff

about fortune and courage? Something American, biblical?
When they arrive at home plate, this slow-moving foursome,
the helpers stand back, and one hands the boy

a bat, about half the usual size. Then the umpire lowers
the tee, and everything's strangely back on track:
the concession line starts moving again, the outfielders chat,

the duck that wandered into the bleachers
finds its way to the shady pond. That's when
I hear from the rows down in front a few people

shouting, *Come on, Tim!* Or is it *Tom?* I can't tell
from watching if Tim or Tom hears them, but then confidence,
like happiness, doesn't always need to be coaxed.

The kid who runs for the boy who can't—he knows this,
and waving to the cheering strangers,
heads for second as if he were that very boy.

. . .

On a Stanza by Rilke

Difficult, isn't it?, to love these high-topped
foul-mouthed teens, this baggy threesome
in shorts and T-shirts—a torn one screaming,

as though it were informative or funny, Eat Me!
Sure, each was somebody's baby once—
this Beavis roughhousing with his Butt-head

buddies: chunky look-alikes, wanting
nothing more in the world right now
than to kick some ass in a game of fast-

break Two-on-One. Sometimes energy
has an odor and takes up a lot of space.
Thunk: somebody hits one. And immediately

a single gut-propelled syllable—Yes!—
spins through the gym, then echoes upward,
as if this voice meant to swallow the ceiling

that's higher than a steeple's. Next door,
in fact, they're actually building one—
or trying to. There's a half-done shell

and, on the grass, a huge bell by a sign
that says: Future Home of Grace Church.
Curiously, the makers are also believers:

I overheard one of them at a garage sale,
telling how he'd brought his family from Texas
to give his "brethren" a hand. They're not

. . .

the only ones, either; when I see them all
out there, during the day, measuring or carrying
or pounding on something, the parking lot's

crowded with silver trailers and cars
with out-of-state plates. Yes, the man said,
they were happy here thus far. So in that

they're like these boys: still strangers
to their grown-almost-to-adult-size bodies,
but pleased, why not?, with what

they've learned. Like the best way to hang
from a rim without snapping it, to slap the creaking
backboard as they test their newfound strength.

Do they feel like Supermen? Well, good for them—
but something still urges me to invoke the rules,
report them on the sly the way I did some-

times at practice: how else to get back at the one
who bullied me, the one who threatened
to piss in my mouth during showers?

Well, life's vulgar, I hear my eighth-grade coach say.
And isn't it? In the training room,
I put on the headphones that sing to me:

relax, and later, *pump up!,* and then a group
of preschoolers wanders into the gym,
assembled under watchful eyes. Whose?

—Camp-leader's? Baby-sitter's? Teacher's?
The hoops to these kids are higher than heaven,
so they roll a ball on the floor. And the teens

go off hungry to raid the machines,
to bang on the TV stashed under a counter
in the so-called supervisor's office: it's hard

. . .

not to judge them harshly, though my own son's
almost their age. There are too many people
in the world. As for the faithful, raising the church—

who'll struggle soon with that bell it takes
a two-story crane to lift—is it true what we
like to believe? That *for them existence*

is still enchanted. Still beginning
in a hundred places. A playing of pure powers
no one can touch and not kneel to and marvel.

. . .

Notes

"On a Stanza by Rilke" concludes by adapting several lines from A. Poulin Jr.'s translation of *The Sonnets to Orpheus.*

"Walkie-Talkie" is for David Henry.

"The Problem" and "Spilled It" reconfigure some passages from *Edie* by Jean Stein.

"City of Men" is for Mary and Ed.

"Go" is for Suzanne Schnackenberg.

"Ampersand," for Ann Murphy, adapts several phrases from *Beyond the Brillo Box* by Arthur C. Danto.

. . .